The
Easter Women

The Easter Women
Luke 7:36–8:3; 23:55–24:12; John 20:1–
18 for children

Written by Carol Greene
Illustrated by
Betty Wind

ARCH®BOOKS

Copyright © 1987 Concordia Publishing House
3558 S. Jefferson Avenue, St. Louis, MO   63118-3968
Manufactured in the United States of America

As Jesus went traveling from village to town,
Teaching and showing God's ways,
Some men (there were twelve)
    walked along with the Lord;
They helped, and they learned and gave praise.

But not only men followed Jesus on earth;
Women believed in Him, too.
Some helped from their homes,
    and some traveled along,
Doing everything that they could do.

There was Mary, His mother; Salome another;
And Mary the mother of James,
Joanna, Susanna, and quite a few more
Who helped (but we don't know their names).

Mary of Magdala followed Him, too,
Though once she had been very bad.
From seven demons her Lord set her free;
So He was the best Friend she had.

Once at a party, she fell on her knees
And washed Jesus' feet with her tears.
She dried with her hair, anointed them too.
The host watched with self-righteous sneers.

"This woman is wicked," he said to himself,
"And Jesus cannot even see."
But Jesus *could* see—inside the man's mind.
"Now, Simon, you listen to Me.

"When I arrived, you did nothing for Me,
No water, no oil, and no touch.
But *this* woman loves Me with all of her heart.
You see, I've forgiven her much.

So Mary of Magdala
        knew the Lord's peace;
It sang in her heart
        like a song.
When the Lord said, "Let's go
        to Jerusalem now."
She packed up
        and went right along.

But there in the city, whispers grew loud.
Such terrible things people said!
When Mary heard them, her peace flew away.
The song in her heart turned to dread.

"Could they kill Jesus?" she wondered aloud.
"Can such ugly rumors be true?"
No one could answer, no one could say,
Because they were wondering too.

A Friday it was when she and her friends
Watched as a cross split the sky.
On it hung Jesus, the true Son of God.
They watched—and they saw Jesus die.

How empty they felt as they stumbled away
And went to fix spices . . . and cry.
"I now will anoint Him again," Mary thought,
"But this time—oh, why did He die?"

They went with their spices out to the tomb
On Sunday, just before dawn.
"The stone is rolled back! No one is here!"
The body of Jesus was gone.

To Peter and John,
        who were Jesus' good friends,
They ran with their hearts beating hard.
"Someone took Jesus! His body is gone!
Oh, what have they done with our Lord?"

Off to the tomb hurried Peter and John.
Mary came panting behind.
The men went on in . . . but she stood alone,
Wondering what they would find.

They found the new linens
  they'd used for His wrap,
But forgot what the Scriptures had said.
His body was gone, but they didn't believe
That Jesus was no longer dead!

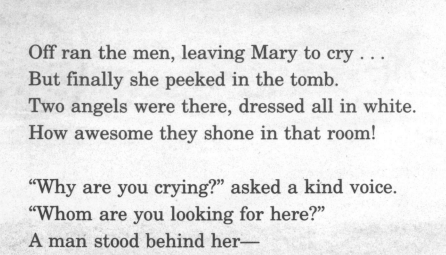

Off ran the men, leaving Mary to cry . . .
But finally she peeked in the tomb.
Two angels were there, dressed all in white.
How awesome they shone in that room!

"Why are you crying?" asked a kind voice.
"Whom are you looking for here?"
A man stood behind her—
    the gardener perhaps?—
Poor Mary; her eyes were not clear.

"Mary!" He called her. And then Mary knew.
"Rabonni! My teacher!" she said.
"Don't touch me," He said;
    "tell the others I live!"
So back through the streets Mary fled.

The song in her heart soared up like a bird.
She heard it again and again.
"Jesus the Savior has trampled down death.
He lives! Alleluia! Amen!"

DEAR PARENTS:

Of all of Jesus' disciples, Mary Magdalene was the first to see the risen Lord (Mark 16:9). Mary responded in awe and joy and then in obedience and witness: she "went and said to the disciples, 'I have seen the Lord' " (John 20:18 RSV).

Mary, most likely from the town of Magdala on the southwest shore of the Sea of Galilee, from which she derives her name, joined Jesus' immediate family of followers near the beginning of His Galilean ministry. Like Joanna and Susanna, Mary helped support Jesus and His disciples and "provided for them out of [her] own means" (Luke 8:3).

Luke also tells us that Jesus cast out of Mary "seven demons"; she responded to her Master's love, not only with her "means, " but also with a bold witness and a life of faith. Along with the apostle John and some of the other women who followed Jesus, she did not desert her Savior at His crucifixion: "Standing by the cross of Jesus were His mother, and His mother's sister, Mary the wife of Clopas, and Mary Magdalene" (John 19:25). Brave Peter and most of Jesus' beloved followers were nowhere in sight.

Share with your child the joy of Mary's Easter discovery, for Mary's Savior—and ours—has arisen indeed and has won each of us "from all sins, from death, and from the power of the devil."

The song in her heart soared up like a bird.
She heard it again and again.
"Jesus the Savior has trampled down death.
He lives! Alleluia! Amen!"

THE EDITOR